Original title:
The Deep's Secret

Copyright © 2025 Creative Arts Management OÜ
All rights reserved.

Author: Giselle Montgomery
ISBN HARDBACK: 978-1-80587-411-9
ISBN PAPERBACK: 978-1-80587-881-0

Whispers of the Abyss

In the ocean's chair, an octopus grinned,
He had tales of clams, but none would be pinned.
A crab wore a crown, quite out of his shell,
He claimed he was king, but the throne? A good swell.

Fish played charades, with bubbles for talk,
A dolphin dove deep, said, "I've got the flock!"
The sea cucumbers laughed, laid back in dismay,
While seaweed would dance, as if ready to sway.

Shadows Beneath the Waves

A sunken ship hosted a fishy debate,
About mermaids' tales and their terrible fate.
Jellyfish floated, with lights on each tentacle,
They dazzled the sharks, which was quite a spectacle.

A turtle in sunglasses cruised the deep tides,
Claimed he once raced against the moon's bright rides.

Treasures in the Silent Blue

In the sunken chest lived a grumpy old eel,
His treasure was junk – a rusted old wheel.
He shouted at crabs trying to steal his loot,
But all they could find was one very lost boot.

A pirate fish searched for the fabled gold,
But found only shells and a story retold.

Secrets of the Midnight Current

At midnight, the currents hatched jokes from the sand,
A narwhal shared puns like he had a big brand.
The sea stars giggled, stuck on the reef's floor,
While the anglerfish sighed, "I won't bait anymore!"

A playful old whale swam round and around,
Outsmarted by plankton that turned him around.

The Ocean's Hidden Heart

Bubbles rise like giggles, oh what a sight,
Fish wear hats, dancing in the moonlight.
Corals hum songs, a quirky parade,
Octopus juggles shells, in shades of jade.

Crabs tap dance, their claws keep the beat,
Seaweed sways gently, it's quite the treat.
With a wink of a whale, a splash of delight,
The ocean's so silly, it's love at first sight.

Murmurs from the Depths

Whispers from fishes, secrets so grand,
Sharks play tag, in this watery land.
A dolphin forgets, he's supposed to dive,
Instead, he spins tales, making waves come alive.

A clam tells a joke, with pearls for its laughs,
While starfish are giggling, writing their drafts.
With treasure maps leading to jellyfish pies,
You'd think the ocean's filled with silly surprise!

Beneath the Surface's Veil

Anemones giggle at turtles that glide,
As crabs hold their breath, to slide down a tide.
With plankton in tuxedos, and clowns in ballet,
The nautical circus is here for the day!

A narwhal sings solo, off-key as can be,
While sea cucumbers dance with glee.
In this underwater cabaret so free,
You'll laugh till you're gilled, come swim and see!

Echoes of Forgotten Tides

Seahorses play leapfrog, oh what a game,
With barnacles cheering, they all feel the fame.
A riddle from a pufferfish, bursting with cheer,
"Why did the shrimp refuse to share its beer?"

The waves chuckle softly, as they sway and tease,
With fish wearing sunglasses, they swim with ease.
Every splash and each ripple holds laughter untold,
These oceanic whispers are treasures of old.

Depths that Speak

Bubbles rise with tales to tell,
Fish gossip, sounding like a bell.
Clams just grin, they know too much,
Underwater drama, what a touch!

An octopus winks, it's quite the tease,
Whispers float through kelp-like trees.
Crabs dance awkward, in a conga line,
While plankton roll on, feeling fine!

Starfish argue who's the star,
From coral palaces, they travel far.
Laughs echo through seashell halls,
Everyone's merry, despite the squalls!

And as the waves softly sway,
The ocean laughs at the light of day.
What secrets lurk beneath the blue?
Only the fishes truly knew!

Tantalizing Tides

Waves do a jig, with sand in tow,
Seagulls squawk, a raucous show.
Mermaids giggle as they dive,
In bubbly worlds where all's alive!

Surfboards dance on frothy curls,
while whales serenade with bubbles and swirls.
Clowns of the sea wear rubbery shoes,
Splashing about, they sing the blues!

A crab with shades takes sun in style,
While fish in tuxes swim the aisle.
With shrimp on deck serving tasty fries,
The ocean party never dies!

So grab a drink and join the fun,
Under the sea, we dance 'til sun.
The tides keep teasing, what can it be?
A carnival deep and oh so free!

Kraken's Lament

In a deep dark pit, where squids do pout,
Lurks a kraken who's feeling left out.
"I just want a friend!" it gives a sigh,
But boats sail away, oh my, oh my!

With eight long arms, it tries to wave,
But sailors just scream, brave or knave.
"I'm not here to scare, just want to play,
Can't anyone stay for a rad buffet?"

Gill friends giggle, saying "Not today!"
"This kraken," they chant, "is quite the cliché."
But in its heart, there's giggles galore,
If only they'd knock on its underwater door!

So here it waits, with clams for friends,
Dreaming of parties that never ends.
With whispers of laughter in currents so strong,
The kraken just hums a silly song!

Echoes of the Forgotten Voyage

Lost ships sing with creaks and groans,
Echoing secrets in salty tones.
Ghostly sailors, with laughter so light,
Still roam the seas, day and night!

A parrot squawks, "We've lost the map!"
While barnacles nod, caught in their trap.
"Where's the treasure?" they all demand,
But it's just barnacle soup in hand!

With nets full of thoughts, they fish for dreams,
While jellyfish bob, bursting at seams.
They toast with coral, their glasses raised,
To forgotten voyages, forever praised.

So sail away, on currents so bold,
Where shadows of laughter forever unfold.
In the ocean's depths, where stories dance,
We find the whimsy in fate's own chance!

Treasures We Cannot See

Under the waves, treasures sleep,
Goldfish hold secrets, theirs to keep.
A pirate's hat floats by with a glee,
Waving hello, just to tease me.

Jellybeans grow on coral reefs,
While sea cucumbers provide us laughs.
Oh, the wonders that we cannot see,
Just waving fish in a giggly spree.

Murky Depths and Shimmering Hopes

In waters murky, do crabs wear hats?
They sidestep sideways, like silly bats.
Anglerfish chuckle in dimmed glow,
Swapping stories that no one knows.

A whale sings jokes that echo wide,
While octopuses chuckle fish aside.
In darkness, laughter sparkles like soap,
With bubbles of giggles and glimmers of hope.

Charting the Uncharted

Maps made of jelly and compass of cheese,
Sailors get lost, laughing with ease.
Fish in bow ties swim briskly past,
Saying, 'These currents are a blast!'

Plotting new routes with a wink and a nudge,
A mermaid grins, gives a mischievous drudge.
Every splash tells a story, oh what fun,
The ocean's adventure has just begun!

Lurking Legends of the Abyss

Tales of monsters, grown tall and wide,
But they just want friends, away they hide.
A kraken with socks that don't quite match,
Laughing aloud in a carefree dispatch.

With each legend that bubbles up bright,
Squids doing dances in the soft moonlight.
They're not here to scare, but to share and play,
In the abyss, it's a land of ballet!

The Silence of the Deep Blue

A fish in a hat, he swam with flair,
Telling jokes to the crustaceans there.
They rolled on the sand, laughing with glee,
While jellyfish giggled, floating wild and free.

An octopus juggled with shells and a shoe,
He winked at the turtles, "Can you do this too?"
They cheered and they clapped with a splash and a cheer,
For the show of the sea brought them laughter and beer!

A whale dressed in stripes joined the comical spree,
"Why don't oysters share? They're too shellfish, you see!"
They all burst in laughter, bubbles up in the air,
As the seaweed danced, the humor laid bare.

So if you dive down where the light doesn't gleam,
You'll find the sea's laughter, like a good happy dream.

Beneath the Wave's Lament

A clam told a tale of a pearl on the run,
"He hid in a crevice, just trying to have fun!"
She snickered and sighed, her lips in a pout,
"He never quite learned what not to talk about."

A sardine in stripes tried to break from the school,
"I just want to dance, that should be the rule!"
But the anchovies laughed at his fanciful plea,
"A fish with a dream? Now that's quite a spree!"

The tide took a turn, and the seaweed would sway,
While the starfish composed an odd cabaret:
"Life under the waves can be quite a delight,
Unless you get caught in a fisherman's sight!"

And so down below, where the sun rarely shines,
The fish swap their tales over platters of brine.

Fables of the Ocean Floor

A lobster once dreamed he could play saxophone,
But his pinchers were too clumsy, he played alone.
The shrimp held their sides, they laughed 'til they cried,
While the sea cucumbers rolled, their joy unplied.

A crab made a hat from a floating old shoe,
He strutted about, causing quite a hullabaloo.
"Tell me not to dance!" he proclaimed with a grin,
As he shuffled and jived, letting laughter begin.

An eel wore sunglasses, cool as can be,
"I'm the star of the night, can you not see me?"
But the fish in the shadows just rolled their fishy eyes,
"An eel in shades? What a fishy disguise!"

In the depths of the sea, where the odd is routine,
Their stories are silly, yet always serene.

Reflections in the Abyss

A pufferfish puffed, trying hard to look round,
But the other fish giggled, they made funny sounds.
"If only you're sharp, just like me!" said a bass,
As bubbles of laughter would ripple and pass.

A dolphin who danced showed a flippery flair,
He slipped on a tide and went twirling through air.
"I meant to do that!" he declared like a champ,
With sea turtles chuckling, lighting up like a lamp.

The sand spoke in whispers, with grains full of jest,
As the fish shared their stories, they laughed with the best.
"So what if the ocean's a wavy delight?"
They found joy in the depths, pure and bright.

With a wink and a wave, they were ready for fun,
In the ocean's great theater, the laughter's not done!

Submerged Truths in Saltwater Dreams

In the ocean, fish wear hats,
While jellyfish dance, they're acrobats.
A clam attempts to tell a joke,
But the crab just scoffs and chokes on smoke.

Octopus plays cards with a whale,
Yet he cheats and hopes not to fail.
Starfish is the dealer—so precise,
But who knew sea life can be so nice?

A seahorse writes poetry with flair,
While sea turtles boast of their great hair.
The starry sky flips the ocean blue,
And the sea-horse giggles—who knew?

Bubbles rise like laughter in the tide,
As dolphins surf with joy and pride.
A mermaid sings of fishy tales,
We giggle at her soggy scales.

The Secrets of Sunken Hopes

Beneath the waves, lost treasures gleam,
But squids just want to ride a beam.
The parrotfish and clownfish meet,
"Who's the funniest?" is their sweet fleet.

The anchor sighs, it's feeling old,
While barnacles think themselves quite bold.
The shipwreck laughs, it's true, it seems,
In rusty parts of sandy dreams.

Dolphins play hide-and-seek with glee,
While seaweed whispers secrets free.
A mermaid trips over her own tail,
Sinking down with a comic wail.

Corals gossip about fishy news,
While crabs strut in their fancy shoes.
The ocean floor is one big jest,
With merriment as its grand quest.

Harmony of the Abyssal Night

Beneath the moon, the waters glow,
As clams tell knock-knock jokes in tow.
A fish tries to do a silly dance,
While turtles join in, giving it a chance.

Shimmering lights and swirling glares,
Create a party that no one shares.
The anglerfish shines but doesn't care,
It's just a light for fish who dare.

An octopus plays the saxophone,
While sharks hum along in a deep tone.
Seahorses twirl in their own delight,
All sharing laughter through the night.

Fins and tails whip through the air,
Creating joy beyond compare.
Bubbles float with giggles galore,
As friendships grow forevermore.

Whispers of the Lost Ones

In the currents, we hear their laughs,
Those lost ones sharing silly gaffes.
A ghostly anglerfish says boo,
But it mostly frightens the shrimp crew.

A ship's bell clangs, but who gives a toss?
When sea urchins play toss with a gloss.
The shells all giggle at secrets kept,
As krill in silence just spuriously crept.

Beware the tales of the deep blue,
Where echoes of silliness break through.
The sea's a stage, a comic display,
With wise old turtles holding sway.

As the tides turn in a cheeky laugh,
An octopus juggles, what a gaffe!
With every ripple, the humor flows,
In depths where no one truly knows.

Sirens of the Hollow Sea

In hollow waves, the fish sing high,
With soggy socks, they flutter by.
A tuna with a tutu spins,
While clam shells chatter, gossiping fins.

The kraken's feet, all tangled in lace,
Waltz awkwardly, a jiggly chase.
Octopus plays the banjo, oh so cool,
While mermaids giggle, breaking the rule.

A dolphin, knotted, swims in a loop,
Chasing sea cucumbers, what a goof troop!
The seaweed sways but starts to tease,
With ticklish currents, it swirls with ease.

So join in the frolic, let's make a splash,
In this jolly sea where waves dance and thrash.

Beneath the Veil of Water

Bubbles bubble, fish on parade,
With popcorn shrimp and a crab charade.
Coral castles, funny and bright,
Ocean's jesters, what a silly sight!

Anemones sway, doing the twist,
While jellyfish poke, can't resist!
The starfish claps, but wait, what's that?
A lobster wearing a silly blue hat!

Whales joke about their last big dive,
"Did you hear? A dolphin finally arrived!"
They giggle and rumble through the sea floor,
As goldfish flash secrets they can't ignore.

A treasure chest, full of lost socks,
Pirate parrots squawk, stealing the flocks.
In the veil of waves, with laughter and cheer,
Adventure awaits; come, take a peek here!

Masks of the Cursed Waves

Masked fish swim, in costumes so bright,
A puffer-pirate gives quite the fright.
A crab with glasses, not to be missed,
Leads a parade—oh, watch that twist!

The sea cow giggles, flicking its tail,
While fishes wear hats with a bold, fuzzy trail.
A seahorse juggles, what a strange show,
As waves crash laughter, letting it flow.

A treasure chest burps, what could it hold?
A yeasty bagel, or gems that are gold?
Mermaids toss shells like they're frisbees,
While sardines wiggle, begging for cheese!

In this watery fun, clownfish burst forth,
With bubbles and jokes from the sea's great north.
So pull off your mask, if you dare to play,
In the realm of the waves, come frolic away!

Secrets Whispered by the Wind

The wind has tales of fish with flair,
A blowfish caught in a tangled affair.
Seahorses giggle, tails in a knot,
As the sea breeze whispers, "Give it a shot!"

Crabs hold auditions for a dance show,
While air and waves put on quite the glow.
A clam sings low, with a lazy refrain,
Tickling the surface, they laugh in vain.

With kites made of kelp, up in the blue,
Even the octopus joins the crew!
The waves clap their hands, beneath the sun's ray,
As secrets float about, whisking worries away.

So join in the mirth, let your spirit soar,
In this wind-whipped world, there's laughter galore.
From tales of the tide to breezes that blend,
In nature's funny play, the fun never ends!

Secrets Buried in Coral

In coral beds, fish hide away,
Where seaweed dancers twist and sway.
A crab with shades has quite the flair,
He winks, then scuttles without a care.

The octopus wears a hat of foam,
Sipping seaweed tea, he's never alone.
He whispers jokes to fish in blue,
They giggle and shoal, just a quirky crew.

Anemones wave in their flowery gown,
While starfish just lounge, the kings of the town.
A dolphin flips with a sly little grin,
A secret, no doubt, let the ocean begin!

Bubbles rise from a clam's tiny lips,
The gossip is juicy, oh, the scoops and quips!
They giggle at sailors and their lost socks,
In this ocean wonder, anything rocks!

Veil of the Abyss

Beneath the waves where shadows play,
A turtle spins tales of yesterday.
He rolls his eyes at humans' fears,
While sipping kelp tea and chuckling cheers.

A squid in disguise, with ink as his shield,
Writes funny notes that the fishes all wield.
They pass them around like a game of charades,
As laughter erupts in the watery glades.

The anglerfish grins with his lure aglow,
Lighting up jokes in a dim, fishy show.
He hooks all the puns like a master of tricks,
While ocean-goers cackle and wiggle their fins.

Coral reefs giggle, they giggle and sway,
As secrets ensue at the end of the day.
With seashells for helmets, the crabs take their stance,
In the deep, dark abyss, they all love to dance!

Murmurs from the Ocean Floor

Down in the depths where the secrets reside,
A sea cucumber does the cha-cha with pride.
With a squishy little shimmy, he steals the show,
Throwing seaweed confetti, oh what a glow!

A shrimp tells a tale, a fishy affair,
Of a whale who thought he could dance in mid-air.
They bark with delight, these underwater geeks,
Sharing the laughter for days and for weeks.

Seahorses sway in their elegant rows,
While snails tell of conch shells with glamorous bows.
They giggle and nudge, "Just wait till you see,
What the snapper will wear to the next jubilee!"

With sand as their seat, they listen and cheer,
The whispers of crustaceans, so vibrant and clear.
Beneath mischievous waves, the laughter is more,
A world of humor from the ocean floor!

Enigma of the Tides

Waves crash with laughter, secrets untold,
A clam sings a tune that's brash and bold.
He calls out to dolphins with jokes made of foam,
In this wet and wild place, all feel at home.

A riddle of tides, with crabs on a quest,
To find out which fish is the funniest guest.
They gather in circles, comparing their jokes,
While sea turtles smirk at the playful folks.

Eels slip and slide with mischievous glee,
Tickling the barnacles, oh what a spree!
They giggle and wriggle, the tide rolling in,
The mystery deepens, let the humor begin!

In the flow of the currents, they dance and they play,
The enigma unfolds in the light of the day.
For what's life in the ocean, without a good jest?
In the waves' wild embrace, laughter's the best!

The Hidden Currents' Song

In the ocean's playful sway,
Fish whisper tales of their day.
Seahorses giggle with glee,
As jellyfish dance, oh so free.

Octopuses hide their clumsy hands,
While starfish plot in sandy strands.
With bubbles, the guppies gently pop,
Singing secrets that never stop.

The crabs do the cha-cha on the floor,
Turtles laugh as they watch the show.
Every wave tells a silly joke,
The sea rolls on, a laughing bloke.

So dive right in, take a splash,
Join the fun, in colorful brash.
The ocean's not just water and sun,
It's a giggling place, oh so fun!

Slumbering Giants Below

In the depths where shadows dwell,
A whale snores like a thunderous bell.
His dreams are filled with tasty krill,
As dolphins giggle, giving a thrill.

An octopus sleeps in a cozy nook,
Tucked in tight with a bedtime book.
With tentacles curled in a comfy curl,
He dreams of prawns and a treasure pearl.

A grouper grumbles, 'No sleep for me,'
With a midnight snack he's swimming free.
While squids with flair, all dressed in ink,
Float down to the ocean's brink.

So if you hear a fishy snore,
Just remember, they're dreaming of more.
In the giant's world, fun never ends,
Where laughter and dreams are very good friends.

Depths of Untold Enigma

What lies beneath the waves so blue?
A riddle wrapped in seaweed's hue.
Cuddly critters in a quirky crew,
Having parties with guests, it's true!

A clam sings opera, a bass plays sax,
Together they form a band with no tracks.
With each swell their music does reach,
A symphony only fishes can teach.

A mermaid giggles in a seaweed throne,
Brushing her hair made of coral stone.
Don't mind the eels; they love to tease,
With wiggly pranks that'll make you wheeze!

So venture down, if fun is your quest,
The ocean's secrets are the very best.
Join the jolly, don't be shy,
In this watery world, let laughter fly!

Beneath the Twilight Waters

The twilight glimmers, the fish all grin,
As turtles toast to the day's sweet spin.
With bubbles of laughter washing ashore,
The crabs hold contests to see who's more.

Beneath the surface, a party unfolds,
With glow-in-the-dark tales and stories bold.
A clownfish juggles with shells and charm,
While eels twist in shapes that alarm!

The roly-poly plankton groove in sync,
Their dance is the talk of the harbor, so pink.
While shimmerfish twirl, it's a dazzling sight,
In the underwater kingdom, everything's bright!

So come take a dip in this cheery space,
Where giggles and friendship will fill up the place.
In the depths where the fun never fades,
Join the celebration that nature parades!

Tides of Unseen Wonders

A fish wearing glasses swam past,
With a wink of a fin, moving fast.
He claimed to know a treasure grand,
But all he showed was a rubber band.

A crab held a sign that read 'Free Hugs',
While starfish danced, giving cozy shrugs.
They joked about pearls and golden coins,
But all I found were a few old groins.

The octopus swirled in a prancy twist,
Claiming he had a bubble-filled list.
But each item turned out to be a joke,
Like a treasure map drawn in bacon smoke.

At last I saw a shimmering light,
But it turned out to be a disco sight.
Underwater it's silly, there's never a frown,
Just a chorus of giggles from the seaweed town.

Riddles of the Deep Blue

A whale wrote riddles in the sand,
With ink made from jellyfish hand.
He asked, 'What swims without feet?'
But all we found was a lost cleat.

The turtles giggled, playing charades,
While seashells laughed at the jokes they made.
One said, 'What bites but doesn't chew?'
The answer was simple: a sea cucumber, too!

A dolphin jumped high to share a pun,
Said, 'What's a fish's least favorite run?'
It's when they have to swim in threads,
With a needle that knits up their little beds.

The bubbles floated with giddy cheer,
As every fish whispered sweet nonsense near.
In the vastness of deep, where odd things unite,
The laughter echoes, a comical sight.

Beneath Layers of Time

A clam dressed in tweed told tales of old,
How time flows differently, or so he was told.
He shared stories of ships that sank with flair,
But all I saw was a whale with a hair.

Corals chatted about vintage trends,
Like seaweed hats and fashionable fins.
They'd argue for hours over colors bright,
While fish took selfies, swimming delight.

From urchins deep, came a quirky song,
About how the ocean hums all day long.
They claimed it's a concert, with bubbles as guests,
But all we heard were shrimpy protests.

At last, I giggled at a wise old eel,
Who said, 'Time's a whirlpool, that's the deal!'
With laughter we swam through currents and tide,
In layers of joy, where fun could not hide.

Abyssal Whispers

An anglerfish flashed his little light,
'Look for treasure!' he'd giggle with delight.
But when I leaned in for the big reveal,
It was just some algae, what a raw deal!

A pufferfish puffed out a snorty tune,
Proclaiming he'd flown to the sun and the moon.
But his friends just laughed, 'You've lost your mind,
You're still here munching on kelp, oh so blind!'

A ghostly shrimp began to tease,
'I once had a partner who was quite the tease!'
But all they found were echoes of old,
Of fables told in the depths bold.

In the depths, the whispers formed a rap,
Jellyfish breakdanced in a fancy cap.
With giggles and wiggles in the ocean's embrace,
Every secret shared felt like a warm grace.

Lurking in the Dark Waters

In the shadows where eels like to dance,
A fish wore a hat and took a chance.
He juggled some pearls, oh such a sight,
While crabs cheered him on, all filled with delight.

A lobster with glasses started to read,
An octopus snored, on seaweed he'd feed.
They played a good game of hide and seek,
Until a whale laughed, causing chaos and squeaks.

The seahorses twirled in a watery waltz,
While clams laughed so hard, they made quite the faults.
Then came a mermaid with bubblegum bliss,
Said, "Join in my show, you won't want to miss!"

So under the waves, where the wackiest dwell,
Life's richer than treasure, it casts quite the spell.
A party of giggles, where fish share their woes,
In the murky abyss, where absurdity flows.

Mysteries of the Sunken Realm

In a castle of coral, the fish held a ball,
With sea turtles twirling, they danced down the hall.
A clownfish came dressed, what a sight to behold,
In a sparkly outfit made of seashells and gold.

The jellyfish floated with grace, oh so fine,
Saying, "Have you seen my lost bottle of wine?"
While sea stars sang tunes, a chorus so bright,
Their harmony echoed through the soft moonlight.

A whale tried to waltz, but ended in knots,
He tripped on a sponge, and landed on pots.
The crowd burst in laughter, what a spectacle!
In the depths, even blunders seem quite mythical.

The treasures of laughter were hidden, not gold,
As seahorses giggled, their antics untold.
In this quirky domain, where odd creatures dwell,
Mysteries unfold, as they cast their own spell.

Chasms of Time and Tide

Once in a canyon of shimmering blue,
A fish told a tale that nobody knew.
He claimed he had met a wise old cod,
Who recited some poems under a seaweed pod.

The turtles were rolling with laughter and cheer,
While anchovies danced, scratching their ear.
They wiggled and giggled at stories so strange,
As a sand dollar's prank made them all rearrange.

With bubbles of giggles rising above,
A grouper proclaimed, "I'm the one who won love!"
But all was in jest, as the chorus broke out,
With fish in a tangle, all wriggling about.

In these chasms of laughs, where time cannot flow,
The rhythm of joy is a vibrant tableau.
For in every tide, there's an echoing sound,
Of funny fish tales, in laughter they're found.

Veiled Depths of Mystery

In the veiled abyss where the weird do convene,
A shrimp wore a tux, feeling quite like a queen.
The pufferfish chuckled, round as can be,
"Surprise! I'm not just a snack, look and see!"

Squids played charades with a flair most divine,
While starfish looked on, drinking seaweed wine.
A dolphin flipped high, announcing with glee,
"Join my comedy show, come and see me!"

With gales of laughter bouncing 'round like a tune,
The depths were alive, like a behind-the-scenes cartoon.
A kraken sang low, as he juggled a sail,
While fish joined the chorus, tipping their scales.

In the veiled world beneath where weird stories thrive,
Laughter's the treasure that keeps tales alive.
For within all the bubbles and wit swirling 'round,
The mystery of joy is the heart's richest sound.

Depths of the Whispering Waters

Bubbles rise, giggling fish,
Chasing dreams of a tasty dish.
Clams play cards, hats on their shells,
Underwater jokes, no one tells.

Octopus dances, limbs in the air,
He's got moves, we just can't compare.
Crabs applaud in their little homes,
While turtles giggle, spinning like drones.

Seahorses gossip, twirling around,
Making up stories that aren't profound.
Jellyfish float, they're just too cool,
Stinging their friends, by the old sea pool.

Eels in tuxedos, so well-dressed,
Invite fish to a shindig, no jest.
Laughter echoes in the azure deep,
As squids share tales before they sleep.

Untold Histories of the Undersea

Treasure chests, not filled with gold,
But socks and spoons, a sight to behold.
Mermaids laughing, brushing their hair,
Finding lost things, in a silver snare.

Sharks in bow ties, suave and chic,
Discussing fish diets, oh so unique.
Starfish claim they're the sun's best friend,
While sea cucumbers munch on the trend.

Giant squids spinning tales so tall,
"Did you see that ship?" they laugh and call.
But fish just shrug, it's all in good fun,
Who needs a ship when you have the sun?

A whale tells stories, deep in the blue,
Of a crab who thinks he's a kangaroo.
With every splash, the laughter flows,
Like bubbles rising, where the current goes.

Mysteries of Sunken Seas

A shipwreck lies with a pirate's cap,
Covered in barnacles, a vintage map.
The crabs hold meetings, all very grand,
Discussing treasure on a sandy strand.

Shy fish peek, through the porthole tight,
Watching the party, what a delight!
Seagulls swoop by, playing pranks on the dive,
While clowns of the ocean sing to survive.

The anchor's a monster, they all agree,
It snored all night, then stole their tea.
Flotsam and jetsam, what a great crew,
Rumors of treasure, is it really true?

Lobsters in suits, feeling quite foxy,
Battling snails who are oh-so-boxy.
A treasure map made of seaweed thrash,
Who will find it first, in a gleeful dash?

Echoes of Forgotten Sailors

Old boats whisper secrets of tides,
As fish in hats ride on the slides.
Sailors once brave, now in a daze,
Befriend dolphins, in a fishy haze.

Ghosts of seagulls, flapping their wings,
Mimic the tales of mermaids' flings.
"Yo ho ho!" they chant with a cheer,
While jellybeans float, oh what a sphere!

Lost nets tickle the octopus toes,
As he giggles softly, nobody knows.
Shimmering whispers of echoed delight,
Enticing all critters to dance through the night.

Forgotten laughter from beneath the waves,
Where creatures gather in glimmering caves.
Tales intertwined, with a splash and a spin,
In the jolly old depths, let the fun begin!

Coordinates of the Forgotten

There's a map with a snicker,
Lost treasure, it says, brings a kicker.
X marks the spot, or is it a cat?
Let's find out, maybe a friendly rat!

In these waters, fish wear glasses,
They gossip about all their classes.
They dance the cha-cha, fins in a twirl,
Who knew sea life could be such a whirl?

An octopus guides with a wink,
His eight arms dance, what do you think?
Bubbles rise up, so full of cheer,
Join the party, don't be a deer!

So grab a snorkel and dive just right,
With laughs and smiles, we'll take flight.
Forget all worries, it's time to play,
In forgotten depths, we'll laugh all day!

Silenced Songs of the Underworld

The fish hold concerts, oh what a sight,
With bubbles as beats, make it feel light.
A clam's the DJ, pearls are his fame,
"Play it again!" the jellyfish claim.

Turtles groove with shells so neat,
While crabs do the shuffle on their small feet.
A sea cucumber sings falsetto high,
"Underwater Idol," gives it a try.

But now and then, a whale pokes in,
With bizarre tunes that make us grin.
"Hey there, buddy, stick to the blues!"
We laugh so hard, we cry out "whoo!"

In depths below, fun does abide,
With all these creatures, we can't hide.
Their silenced songs are now set free,
Dive in the rhythm, come dance with me!

Lighthouses in Darkness

Lighthouses flicker, wearing silly hats,
Warning the ships, just like friendly bats.
"Turn right at the barnacle-covered wall,"
But what if it's just a deep-sea stall?

With beams like disco, they shimmy and sway,
"Watch your fins; don't lose your way!"
A starfish asks, "Is this the right groove?"
As we boat past, we both dance and move.

Squid add confetti, balloons float by,
"Good vibes only!" the seagulls cry.
While dolphins jump in luminous rings,
Their laughter mingles with ocean swings.

So if you're ever lost in the tide,
Look for the lighthouses, don't turn aside.
Just follow the lights and the giggles they send,
For in the dark, fun is a friend!

The Ocean's Silent Confession

In the waves, a secret so grand,
Fish form a choir, oh isn't it planned?
With splashes and giggles, they belt out a tune,
It's a slosh and a gurgle under the moon.

Crabs hold a meeting, oh what a delight,
Planning a feast that lasts through the night.
With sandcastles topped by seaweed hats,
They argue 'bout snacks—sea cucumbers or rats?

Octopuses laugh at their daring schemes,
"I'll juggle your snacks—how about some creams?"
While plankton giggle in shimmering rows,
In these depths, a humor that endlessly flows.

So if you hear whispers from below,
Join the fun, let those giggles grow.
For in the ocean's embrace, take a dive,
And you'll find the joy in being alive!

Beneath the Weight of Blue

Bubbles dance and giggle, oh what a sight,
A fish in a tuxedo, what a delight!
He twirls past the coral, he thinks he's a star,
While seaweed just chuckles, "Look at him, bizarre!"

When turtles wear glasses, they read quite a lot,
Discussing the best spots for a fine, algae pot.
While crabs crack their jokes with a pinch and a snap,
The clownfish just rolls his eyes, takes a nap!

The octopus serves tea, with eight busy hands,
As jellyfish float by with their shimmering bands.
They laugh about humans, so clumsy and loud,
While they sip on their tea, all together, so proud!

Under waves of laughter, echoing glee,
Life beneath the surface is quite quirky, you see.
Each nook holds a party, each bubble a cheer,
Just watch out for sea cucumbers—stay clear!

Wonder in the Stillness

In a quiet lagoon, where the sea meets the sand,
A starfish gives orders, he's quite the demand.
With a seashell on duty, the guards take their post,
While the seaweed just sways, a light-hearted host.

Octopuses juggling, with flair and with grace,
A turtle slow claps—'What a wonderful place!'
While anemones giggle, their tickles a blast,
Sunbathing on rocks, good times go so fast!

A crab tells a tale, of a treasure so rare,
While all of the fish stop to laugh and to stare.
They plot and they scheme, in their watery realm,
To find that lost treasure, to seize a new helm!

But when the tide shifts, and the beach is revealed,
The secrets of laughter, they never concealed.
With bubbles to share and jokes full of cheer,
In the stillness of wonder, the fun is quite clear!

The Call of the Forgotten Depths

Down in the depths, where the sea monsters dwell,
There's a dance-off happening—oh, can you tell?
A whale with a boombox, beats booming quite loud,
While shrimp shake it off, they're the life of the crowd!

An old sunken ship, is the stage for this show,
With starfish as spotlights, they twinkle and glow.
A dolphin's the DJ, spinning tunes from the past,
While the seahorses twirl, oh how long will it last?

"Join us!" say the corals, with colors so bright,
"We've got jelly donuts and all kinds of bite!"
The fish crowd around, in a frenzy of fun,
Legends of laughter, now spread as they run.

And when the tide changes, and the party must end,
Each creature remembers, the joy they defend.
In the call of the depths, where the laughter's a blast,
The whispers of fun in the abyss will last!

Echoes in the Silent Blue

In waters so silent, where the fish play their games,
A dolphin quips jokes, by all sorts of names.
It's a giggly affair, with bubbles galore,
While the grouper just snickers, wanting more!

Not far from a kelp bed, a parrotfish sings,
"Who needs a crown when you've got fins with bling?"
An otter rolls over, on a rock near a reef,
While the crabs all unite, with their pinching belief!

With laughter like ripples, the sea turtles partake,
Discussing the best ways to balance a cake.
But when a wave hits, and the fun's thrown asunder,
They just laugh and exclaim, "What a squishy blunder!"

So here's to the bubbles, and the giggles we share,
In the silent blue spaces, with joy everywhere.
A legacy of laughter, in waters so wide,
Echoes of hilarity that no one can hide!

Dark Abyss

In a place where shadows play,
Fish wear hats, they dance all day.
Jellyfish tell jokes with glee,
While seaweed whispers, "Look at me!"

Octopuses with vibrant ties,
Critique the clouds that drift and fly.
Crabs break out in rhyming schemes,
While clam shells clack like silly dreams.

But deep below, the laughter fades,
As merfolk sing their silly parades.
They've lost their keys and found bad puns,
In this abyss, the real fun runs!

So here beneath the rolling waves,
The mystery's how laughter braves.
With every dive, a surprise awaits,
In this dark place where joy creates!

Light Within

A glow that chuckles in the night,
Puns and giggles take to flight.
Lantern fish with tiny lamps,
Invite the others to their camps.

They toast to blunders, slip and fall,
Bubble parties, oh what a ball!
Shiny shells and sand so bright,
Reflecting all that's pure delight.

A chorus of the wise old rays,
Share stories of their clumsy days.
With every splash, a laugh we find,
In this place where joy's entwined!

So let the glimmer guide your way,
To find the fun in every sway.
For in the depths, with all its girth,
Is laughter's light, the heart of mirth!

Beneath the Salt and Spray

A crab who loves to sing out loud,
Sways with the waves, draws quite a crowd.
Frogs dive deep to grab some fun,
While seahorses race, their times are spun.

The tide tickles with salty glee,
As octopus chefs make a fishy spree.
The oysters giggle, trapped in shells,
While clam friends spin their curious tales.

Below the surf, shenanigans abound,
In every nook, funny sights are found.
A dolphin dives, flips through the air,
While fish parade without a care!

So take the plunge, don't be afraid,
In this salty place, joy's parade.
For laughter bubbles from every shore,
In the depths where silliness galore!

Guardian of the Lost Depths

A grumpy old turtle guards the gate,
With a grin so wide, it's hard to hate.
He misplaces shells, and rights the wrongs,
And busts a move to underwater songs.

Mollusks come dressed in vibrant hues,
Arguing over the best of shoes.
The kraken plays cards, but not too fair,
With eight hands working, the stakes ensnare.

But through it all, the laughter flows,
Echoing where the funny fish goes.
For in each twist, a secret's told,
In depths unfathomed, with laughter bold!

So follow the guardian, wise yet spry,
Who knows the joys beneath the sky.
For every jest and playful stride,
Is where the true magic will abide!

Secrets of the Moonlit Tide

Beneath the silver shining glow,
Winks a trapdoor that starts the show.
With starfish clapping on sandy shores,
As bubble blubbers tease the roars.

Turtles twirl like ballerinas,
While plankton glow in shimmying arenas.
The seaweed sways to the nocturnal beat,
As clams break out their finest feat.

Cracking jokes across the swell,
Mermaids giggle, cast their spell.
They chat about the ocean's quirks,
In this humorous land, where nobody lurks.

Share your dreams with the foam and tide,
For hidden wonders do reside.
In laughter and fun, secrets buried wide,
In the moonlit dance, joy's the true guide!

Hidden Depths of Time

In the ocean's embrace, fish gossip at dawn,
Octopuses knitting, while turtles yawn.
Corals in whispers, they giggle and tease,
As sandcastles tumble, like leaves from the trees.

Crabs wear their shells with great pride and flair,
Dancing in circles, with nary a care.
Seagulls above caw, like they're judging the scene,
While clams hold their breaths, all quiet and keen.

A pirate's lost treasure? Just a rusty old hook,
As mermaids chuckle, with tales in their nook.
Time's tick-tock echoes, with bubbles of glee,
In depths of the water, where jests roam free.

So, come take a plunge, where the laughter stays bright,
In the hidden depths, where the silliness bites.
A world full of pranks, in the teal and blue,
Just watch your step; they've made a big stew!

Currents of the Lost

Down where the currents twist and twine,
Fish with sunglasses, having a fine dine.
They catch the silliest, splashy affairs,
With seaweed confetti and jellyfish chairs.

An old shoe floats by, once someone's lost pride,
Now it hosts a party where all fish reside.
With clam shells for drums and a starfish's cue,
They boogie all night, oh, who knew they'd do?

Dolphins spin tales, though they seem quite absurd,
Of treasure chests filled with the laughter they heard.
Eels twist and shout, the sea's own rock band,
While shrimp do the tango, like this was all planned.

So join in the currents, where the fun just won't stop,
In waters so lively, where giggles will pop.
What's lost isn't gone, it's all just a game,
In these quirky currents, no one's ever the same!

Veils of Foam and Mystery

Under clouds of foam, secrets swirl in delight,
Crabs dressed as kings have a ball every night.
Sea cucumbers gossip in whispers so sly,
While starfish stretch wide, reaching out to the sky.

Underwater tickles, in bubbles they gleam,
Shrimps poke their heads out, just living the dream.
With laughter and riddles, they tease every foe,
In veils of the ocean, where all foolishness flows.

What's hidden from view? Just a crab in a hat,
Conducting the symphony, with chatters and spat.
With sponges and treasures, they dance and they sway,
In waves made of giggles, where silliness stays.

So dive with no worries, come hop on the fun,
For veils can be playful, when the day's nearly done.
In waters that shimmer, there's magic to see,
In the foam where the laughter swims wild and free!

Lighthouses in the Abyss

In shadows so deep, where the sea critters dwell,
Lighthouses giggle, casting jellybean spells.
They shine with a wink, sending fish on their quest,
While barnacles cheer, saying, 'We are the best!'

With beams made of laughter, they beckon the lost,
Fish making cast nets, and nothing's the cost.
Anemones strut, with their polka-dot flair,
While sharks join the dance, surprisingly rare!

In the abyss so wild, with shenanigans planned,
A crab popping confetti, the king of this land.
And as bubbles rise up, it's party on low,
When the lighthouses giggle, the whole ocean glows.

So come take a look at this whimsical place,
Where everything's funny, at a leisurely pace.
In lighthouses bright, where the fun won't dismiss,
Join the dance of the depths, in this laughter-filled bliss!

Depths of Forgotten Dreams

In the ocean, fish wear hats,
And jellyfish dance on silver mats.
Octopuses play a game of tag,
While sea turtles boast of their latest brag.

Coral reefs giggle with each wave,
As crabs tell jokes and misbehave.
Starfish ponder the meaning of life,
While sea urchins sharpen their knives.

Waves whisper tales of underwater lore,
As seahorses trot to a festive score.
The chum of laughter fills the sea,
With bubbles of mirth, so carefree!

Who knew the depths were such a blast,
Where time skips and mirth is vast?
Down below, dreams swirl and gleam,
In a world that bursts at the seam.

Treasures of the Midnight Sea

Under the moon, with a shimmer divine,
Mermaids sip tea, while dolphins align.
Pirates sneeze on their gold hoard,
Yet treasure slips from every cord.

Fish in tuxedos swim with flair,
Puffers puff up, unaware of the scare.
Whales tell tales with a deep hearty laugh,
While angelfish pose for their photograph.

A crab with shoes starts dancing the jig,
And eels in bow ties put on quite the gig.
The kelp forest hosts a grand ball,
With clams and scallops just having a ball!

Hark! The sea's got jokes that won't quit,
From sea cucumbers clowning a bit.
Each wave brings joy, a splash in the night,
With laughter that sparkles, sheer delight.

Silhouettes in the Blue

In the blue, where shadows sway,
Fish play hide-and-seek all day.
A lobster wearing a bright red shoe,
Claims he's the star of the ocean crew.

Shrimps on a mission to paint the sea,
With colors that make all the fish agree.
The seaweed giggles as currents sway,
While crabs toss confetti, hooray hooray!

Dolphins dive in synchronized grace,
While squids pull silly faces in this race.
A fish forgot where he tucked his scale,
Chased by tales of a mythical whale.

But down below, it's all in good fun,
With quirky blotches like spots on a bun.
Each silhouette tells a funny tale,
In the dance where laughter won't fail.

Lurking Mysteries of the Trench

Down where light dares not to creep,
A crab named Bob likes to play hide and peep.
Ghostly fish wear costumes galore,
As they throw a bash on the ocean floor.

A flashlight fish lost his glow,
While anglerfish put on a show.
Strange sounds echo, but don't you fear,
It's just the deep making jokes with cheer.

A sea snail spinning surprisingly fast,
Claims he's training for a race at last.
The oddities here are plain to see,
With squids that giggle, oh so free!

In the trench, tales turn into pranks,
With teamwork unseen, they form merry ranks.
So if you dive deep, don't just scream,
Join in the fun, dream a wild dream!

The Hidden Chorus of the Sea

Bubbles whisper tales of joy,
Where tuna dance and dolphins toy.
Octopuses wear silly hats,
While crabs perform in fancy spats.

A clam with dreams of Broadway fame,
Practices lines, but can't remember his name.
Starfish sing off-key so loud,
Their off notes draw quite the crowd.

Seaweed sways to the fishy tunes,
As jellyfish float like funny balloons.
The sea's a stage, with all its quirks,
A splash of laughter in the lurks.

So dive on down, join the fun,
In this orchestra, there's room for everyone.
For beneath the waves, so free and spry,
Laughter bubbles up from where fish fly.

Ripples of Lost World

In the sand, footprints disappear,
As sea turtles giggle, never fear.
A crab with swagger, doing the twist,
Claims he's the king — who'd dare to resist?

Shells conspire to gossip and tease,
About the octopus with eight left feet.
A dolphin slips with a laugh and a dive,
Says, 'I'm the reason the sea's so alive!'

The sunken ships tell stories grand,
Of pirates' dances on this golden sand.
But the fish all know they're just tales of yore,
For the real treasures are the laughs and more.

So splash a bit, let loose and sigh,
In this watery world, where giggles won't die.
The ripples echo with joy so bright,
In the ocean's playground, day turns to night.

Shadows in the Ocean's Embrace

In murky water, shadows prance,
With squid doing the tango, oh, what a chance!
Anglerfish with lights, they're having a ball,
They flash their glow like a disco hall.

The sea cucumber glides with style,
While plankton adds the rhythm with a smile.
"Just don't step on my toes!" they all cheer,
In this underwater party, you have nothing to fear!

A whale sings blues, oh, what a sound!
As turtles sway and the seabed's spun round.
"Let's parade through the reefs, make a stunning display!"

The coral joins in, in a colorful array.

So dive into shadows, let laughter reclaim,
The ocean's embrace is a hilarious game.
Where a flick of a fin can start a parade,
And everyone swims to the music they've made.

Dancer of the Abyss

A fish in a top hat takes center stage,
While the sea life gathers, turning the page.
"Watch my moves!" he proclaims with a wink,
As the audience gasps, then starts to think.

With swirling skirts and a twirling tail,
He pirouettes like he's riding a gale.
The seaweed sways, caught in the thrill,
As the jellyfish join in, showing off skill.

Crustaceans snap their claws with glee,
Joining the dance, a sight to see!
Bubbles rise like confetti in cheer,
Each splash echoing, "Come join us here!"

So plunge into the deep where the dance never ends,
Where laughter and rhythm are steadfast friends.
In the abyss, fun is the only decree,
As each sea critter shakes it, wild and free.

Hushed Voices Beneath the Sea

Bubbles giggle, fish do play,
Whispers dance in currents gray.
Octopus jokes in eight-fold rhyme,
While clams complain about the time.

Starfish winks, a wink so sly,
They argue 'bout who'll fly and why.
Corals chuckle, sway about,
As sea cucumbers laugh out loud.

Secrets Wrapped in Seaweed

A crab with a hat, so very grand,
Tells tales of treasure on golden sand.
Seaweed wraps secrets like a gift,
While fish around start to drift.

Anemones giggle in a funky way,
As turtles show off their ballet.
With every wave, new gossip flows,
Where nobody knows just how it grows.

The Heart of Silent Waters

Fish with a flair, they put on a show,
Pirouetting past seaweed's glow.
Whales hum a tune, oh so sweet,
While squids change colors, no need to cheat.

Mermen chuckle, sipping peach tea,
Plotting their pranks beneath the sea.
Hidden giggles, a bubbling spree,
What a wild, wacky jubilee!

Legends Carried by the Current

A seahorse rides on tales so tall,
As dolphins debate who's best at the ball.
Old anchors sigh, holding on tight,
While shells sing softly to the moonlight.

Mermaids bake cakes with sprinkles bright,
Using starfish as their delight.
The current flows, it hums and sings,
With a sprinkle of laughter, oh, what it brings!

www.ingramcontent.com/pod-product-compliance
Lightning Source LLC
Chambersburg PA
CBHW060145230426
43661CB00003B/582